Voices Bri...

Voices Bright Flags

Geoffrey Brock

WAYWISER

First published in 2014 by

THE WAYWISER PRESS

Bench House, 82 London Road, Chipping Norton, Oxon OX7 5FN, UK
P.O. Box 6205, Baltimore, MD 21206, USA
http://waywiser-press.com

Editor-in-Chief
Philip Hoy

Senior American Editor
Joseph Harrison

Associate Editors
Dora Malech Eric McHenry V. Penelope Pelizzon Clive Watkins Greg Williamson

A CIP catalogue record for this book is available from the British Library

ISBN 978-1-904130-64-2

Printed and bound by
T.J. International Ltd., Padstow, Cornwall, PL28 8RW

For Ravi & Mira

Contents

HOMELAND SECURITY

AMERICAN ORNITHOLOGY

HEADLANDS

Foreword by Heather McHugh

The collection *Voices Bright Flags* could have been created only by a lover of texts – an avid consumer of histories, biographies, diaries, essays, articles, ledgers, novels and ephemera. It is a book *of* and *for* the old-fashioned reader, the one who will appreciate the precise prosodic dados and dove-tailings of the poet's craft.

Many of *Voices Bright Flags'* constituent pieces are dramatic monologues – bringing to life the gestures, sensibilities and allegiances of individuals within variously formative American clans: native American tribes, European explorers and claim-stakers, African-American slaves, sharecroppers and freedmen, Asian settlers, and others who accompanied and succeeded them. The ensemble of these pieces accomplishes a cautionary paean to America itself.

Brock creates a complex social tapestry of the occasions that arouse and beset these cultures. But he also conjures up nature's powerful presences, shaped and shaping – crag and bog; shore and flora; weathers, woodlands and wildlives. (The Wilson and Audubon monologues are as clinically detached as they are circumstantially heartbreaking, and they serve as forms of augury, as well.)

And that is, after all, why we go to art – not merely to admire rhetorical flourish, but to revivify our sense of our own living circumstances, which, in the welter of our days, never seems as clear, or as consequential, as when reflected in another's watchful eye.

Indeed, one cannot read these historical accounts and monologues without the flicker of an insight into our futures. It's a reader's gift to another reader, this foreshadowing of ends, of course: the sense of destinations a reader of worlds can offer to a reader of words (and vice versa).

Brock doesn't preach; he observes and inquires. In whatever cradles of state or predisposition Americans may begin, a poet as scrupulous as he (as alert to the destiny of *lines* as to the destiny of *lives*) finds, along the documentary trail, a collective streaming inclination – enlarged by so many tributaries – to come to our own conclusions.

"It is a complex fate to be an American," Henry James observed.
— James Baldwin

HOUSELIGHTS

Bryant Park at Dusk

The floodlights are on behind and above
    Where I sit in my public chair.
The lawn that had gradually darkened is bright now.
    The library windows stare.

I'm alone in a crowd – e *pluribus plures*.
    I'm far from a family I miss.
I'd almost say I'm lonely, but lonely
    Is worse, I know, than this.

Loneliness is a genuine poverty.
    I'm like a man who is flush
But forgot his wallet on the nightstand
    When he left for work in a rush,

And now must go without food and coffee
    For a few hours more than he'd wish.
That's all. He still *has* a wallet. It's bulging.
    It floats through his brain like a fish…

Money for love: a terrible simile,
    But maybe it's fitting here,
A couple of blocks from Madison Avenue
    Where commodities are dear,

Where all around me, rich skyscrapers
    Woo the impoverished sky,
Having sent on their way the spent commuters
    Who stream, uncertain, by,

And as for this whole splurge of a city,
    Isn't money at its heart?
But I'm blathering now. Forgetting my subject.
    What I meant to say at the start

Is that I've been watching a woman reading
    In a chair not far from mine.
Silver-haired, calm, she stirs a hunger
    Hard for me to define,

Perhaps because she *doesn't* seem lonely.
    And what I loved was this:
The way, when dusk had darkened her pages,
    As if expecting a kiss,

She closed her eyes and threw her head back,
    Book open on her lap.
I guessed she was thinking about her story,
    Or the fall air, or a nap,

And I thought she'd leave me then for pastimes
    More suited to the dark.
But she is on intimate terms, it seems,
    With the rhythms of Bryant Park,

For that's when the floodlights came on, slowly,
    Somewhere far above my need,
And the grass grew green again, and the woman
    Reopened her eyes to read.

About Opera

Fuggirmi io sol non so

In the real world, lighting is undesigned;
here it's high art. After we find our seats,
silence our cells and smooth our ruffled minds,
and just before the curtains rise, houselights

go out. We vanish, and before our eyes
adjust, a splendid spectacle begins
in which we're borne, again, into the lives
of others – figures whose shaded joys and pains

might be, for these three hours, ours. Yet
what can we hope to understand of them?
Words in a strange, old tongue (*il fazzoletto!*)
shine through the wordless music as through a scrim

by turns opaque and blindingly transparent –
words whose sources are masks, mouths gaping wide.
Still, some intelligence like a welder's current
leaps the orchestra pit (where shadows hide

that pulsing drum, those lacerating strings),
and something is spilling, something even grander,
perhaps, than life, from the woman who now sings,
now dies, as passion fills white space around her,

fills us, and tears are spilling down *our* faces –
there's too much light, it's all too brightly lit!
Kind curtains fall, and a governed dark replaces
all light but the glow of the pages in the pit.

Staring Back at Us
(A Gallery)

Angela's Passage: 1619

Jope...brought not any thing but 20. and odd Negroes,
wch the Governor and Cape Marchant bought for victualle.
– John Rolfe

Call her the first. She wasn't alone, but hers
is the name that comes to us. Plucked from a place
somewhere along the banks of the river Kwanza,
then taken to Cape Comfort, in Virginia,

aboard two ships: first the *São João Bautista*,
a Portuguese slaver bound for Vera Cruz,
then an English privateer, the *Treasurer*
(oh bright ironical names), which traded her

for food. Such was her case. Engendered there:
Fort Sumter shelled, Atlanta burned to rubble,
and Abraham Lincoln dead.
                              Its trading done,
her ship set sail, indifferent as a swan.

*

[What use, to us, Leda or Zeus? We've grown
new maids, new gods – Iliums of our own.]

Wheatley in the Tower of London: 1773

On what seraphic pinions shall we move?
– Phillis Wheatley

With Granville Sharp I went to see the Tower.
We gazed upon the crowns of sires and scions
and freely spoke for one undying hour,
but fell to silence at the prisoned lions.

For crowns are signs, and signs are abstract things;
they scarcely stirred the drape on my heart's cage.
Yet when I saw those *creatures*, I felt wings
thrashing inside me, heard the call of rage.

(No other heard, of course; I was a slave
and wise to show a pretty parrot heart.
And none hear now, though I be free to rave,
since I must make a *living* from this art.)

*

[Call her our first poet; she wasn't and was.
But look: enslaved, she was the toast of London.
Free, she couldn't publish her second book
and died a scullery maid at 31.]

The State of Virginia: Christmas 1831

I saw white spirits and black spirits engaged in battle, and the sun was darkened.
— Nat Turner

And now our nights are spent listening to noises,
a farmer writes to his sister. He recalls
watching the messenger's dust-trail hang in the air,
then turning to face the house his father had built,

recalls the blur of his wife in the parlor there,
his son and the cook's boy wrestling on the porch.
A corn song, a hog call, is often the germ
of nervous terror, and a cat in the dining room

will banish sleep for the night. Recalls as well
the mutter of tools and voices from the field,
and dark thin shapes that he could scarcely see,
bending and turning. Now, he dips his pen,

wanting to offer, in closing, some word of wisdom –
but sees his sister's childhood scowl, and so
merely asks again whether Cincinnati
agrees with her, and whether they've had snow.

*

[Facing a thousand tomes on the Civil War
in our local bookshop, my son asks: Why so many
books on a single subject? A long story,
I say. And if there's an end, it's just beginning.]

Day of Settlement: Dec. 2, 1859

I dared not refuse to obey, but at first I did not
strike hard. 'Harder!' he said; 'harder, harder!'
– John Brown, Jr.

We knew the rules and punishments:
three lashes for lack of diligence,
eight for disobeying mother
or telling lies.... *No blood*, he'd say,

and no remission. Came a day
he started keeping my account,
as at a store. And came another
he called me to the tannery:

a Sunday, day of settlement.
I'd paid one-third the owed amount
when he, to my astonishment,
handed the blue beech switch to me,

tearful. (The greatest of my fears:
never his whippings, but those tears.)
And so it was my father paid,
himself, the balance I had owed,

our mingled blood a token of
a thing that went unnamed: his love.
This nation, too, is his bad child.
And she has failed him, made him wild

with rage and grief, and will be scourged
nearly to death before she, purged,
may rise and stand. *No blood*, I hear
him saying still, *and no remission.*

So hang him today, Virginia; cheer
his body swaying in the air –
tomorrow you will learn what's true:
hanging's a thing he's done for you.

*

[Recall who caught him, saw him hanged for treason:
a man named Lee who would make treason look *noble*
(and red war redder) for – well, no good reason.
File under: Looking-Glass World, Lost-Cause Rebel.]

Whitman on Broadway: Apr. 13, 1861

Arous'd and angry, I'd thought to beat the alarum, and urge relentless war,
But soon my fingers fail'd me...
                    – Walt Whitman

He who, fresh from a Verdi opera, was humming
his way down Broadway toward the Brooklyn ferry.
He, who heard the fury of newsboys coming,
their voices, still unbroken, flailing the air,

their midnight extras flapping like gray flags.
He, who had tried to write a *poem*

                              to bind us.
Gathered with others beneath the flaring lamps
of the Metropolitan. Read that news in silence.

                    *

[Instead of all the statues of generals on horses
give me Walt that night at Broadway and Prince
buying a *World* or a *Times* from a barefoot orphan
and trying to make, of the kosmos disorderly, sense.]

William Howard Russell at Bull Run: July 21, 1861

america   as much a problem in metaphysics as
it is a nation
                        – Robert Hayden

They came – men in straw hats and linen coats,
wives with their parasols – in country cars
laden with city wares: with picnic baskets

and opera glasses, with pens for sketching notes.
"Bully for us!" and "Splendid!" and "My stars!"
they cried at the bright flags, the smoke, the muskets.

          (I have seen war. The horror, the sheer mess –
          Balaklava, Sebastopol. But *this*?)

They sipped their tea. Their brandy and Bordeaux.
Then fled like hares from what they too now know.

                        *

[And reenactments – Christ! Bull Run again
six months ago: hundred-degree heat,
each soldier in period wool, with a replica gun
(cheating, perhaps, with ice beneath his hat) –

and this: two sets (just one, through the theurgy
of time, can see the other) of spectators!
As Freud said: first the trauma, then the urge
to rhyme it. Or Marx: first tragedy, then farce.]

Frank Haskell at Gettysburg: July 2, 1863

"There were stern stands / And bitter runs for glory."
– Stephen Crane

The summer heat pressed down, despite the sky's
mizzling rain. We waited, where hours later
the dead would sprawl in scattered ricks, the wounded
would wait like bettors at a ticket office

for amputations. Such things I saw! Cords
of arms and legs. At every house and shed
they lay – the gray-haired men, the beardless boys –
some pleading for the final panacea,

some mute, some glassily polishing tales of victory.
But first: the wait. Between our lines and theirs
lay fields of wheat, soon to be ripe. Between us,
a pasture, a peach orchard, patient corn.

Surgeons readied hospitals, stretchers. Soldiers
loitered. Several I saw curl in the dirt
to sleep. One went for water, twenty canteens
clanking like medals at his neck. Some smoked

and some told jokes and some just blinked like cows.
Then Sickles led his idiot march, and the wait
ended, and fifty thousand ramrods were thugging
their little cones, their little globes of lead…

*

[Engendered too our weird mythologies –
history our Homer (our honer, our harshener):
Uncle Tom whipped to death for his defiance;

or Klansmen, even their horses hooded, racing
to Elsie's aid as *Ride of the Valkyries* blares;
or Scarlett picking cotton to save Tara…]

James Daniel Brock at Cold Harbor: June 3, 1864

What like a bullet can undeceive!
– Herman Melville

My grandfather's grandfather died at 1 AM,
eight hours after a Union minie ball
entered behind his left ear (the letter said)
and ranged up. He had seen his share of slaughter,

but nothing like what he'd have witnessed had he lived
a few more hours: blue-black uniforms
emerging from the cool foreshadows of dawn
wearing the faces of men trying only to die

as men. Pinned to each back: a name and address
on a slip of paper.
                                    By the order to fire,
they'd come so close he would have seen the breaths
of dust, at impact, puffing from their coats.

A few more days, he might have stuffed his nostrils
(many survivors did) with crushed green leaves
as the entrenched living, awaiting further orders,
stared at each other across ripe fields of dead.

*

[Six years it took me to make the time to find
the Confederate cemetery in Fayetteville;
it's a quarter mile from my house in the crow's mind,
but he flies over a private, wooded hill.

On foot, it's down, back up, around a bend
atop a steep road marked (*oh please*) DEAD END.
And why come now, I wondered, as I weaved
among the headstones of the undeceived.]

Monroe's Doctrine: Good Friday, 1865

The shining black mask they wear does not
show a ripple of change; they are sphinxes.
– Mary Boykin Chesnut

Miss Mary's diamonds was hid under Lizzie's apron.
Them Yanks was taking this and breaking that.
They mocked Miss Mary for running to us, then us
for standing by her side, though we was free.

Knowing Miss Mary's mouth, I says to her
"Don't answer back, Miss Mary – just let 'em cuss.
Don't let 'em say that you was impudent."
Them Yanks they laughed at that. But not Miss Mary.

She squinnied at me like I wasn't her Monroe.
Like them old draperies that always hung
in front of her eyes was flung aside, and she
was having trouble adjusting to the light.

Next day we gave them diamonds back like they
was garden peas, and Lizzie and me, we left.

*

[...and old myths taking U-turns: once beloved,
Uncle Tom, like some poor mortal in Ovid
who slights a god, becomes himself a whip;
Tara decays on the Forty Acres backlot

(only the façade was real); and the troops
(integrated now) of Colonel Kilgore
(you know: *the smell of napalm in the morning*)
blast Vietnam with *Birth of a Nation*'s score...]

Grant on His Deathbed: 1885

Nations, like individuals, are punished for their transgressions.
– U.S. Grant

Have never dwelt on errors. On omissions.
Cold Harbor – order for that last assault.
The field of wounded staring back at us.
At me. Helplessly dying. Dreams' projections.

Blamed Lee for thwarting my desire to lessen –
but I, I know, I should have called a truce.
And Vicksburg too. Final attack. At fault.
(What I wanted to be was a professor.)

And that most unjust war – root of it all:
Mexico. Foretaste of command. Recall
with shame that wounded colonel. Unresisting.

My heart then like a puffed-up private boasting
he's cut the enemy's leg off.
                              – Not his head?
– Sir, someone else had cut that off already.

*

[I used to walk up Riverside to his tomb,
and sit across the street, in Sakura Park,
in April, when the cherries were in bloom,
and read, and stare, until it got too dark.]

CONCORDANCES

Seeing Armstrong: Oct. 12, 1931

1.

Charlie Black   was a white boy
     It was nineteen
                thirty-one
The town was Austin   Texas
     Louis Armstrong
               played a horn

The venue   was the Driskill
     Black entered
               through the front door
He played   mostly with his eyes closed
     things that had never
               existed before

Charlie Black   a white boy
     saw a black man
               play a horn
He was the first   genius
     I had ever
           seen

It was nineteen thirty-one   it was Texas
     Black
         was white
Black was   sixteen when he went out
     looking for girls
             that October night

For a Southern   white boy
     can you understand
             what it meant
to see genius for the
         first time in a
     black man?

2.

Linda Brown   was a black girl
     in Kansas
              in fifty-four
John Brown had left the state   *bleeding*
     Kansas
       a century before

Charles Black was now
        a lawyer
    on Thurgood Marshall's team
Linda Brown   was a
        plain black girl
    whose parents had a –

Linda Brown   was Homer Plessy
    her school
        his railway car
Linda Brown was   Dred Scott
    fighting
       the same war

Charlie   Black was a white boy
    back in nineteen
          thirty-one
The road before him   wound
    from Austin
       to beyond

It was then   that I started walking
    toward the Brown case
        where I belonged
The venue was   the Driskill
    Louis Armstrong
       sang a song.

King: Apr. 7, 1968

We brought both babies as to a christening.
– Van K. Brock, "King"

We stood in line for hours to see his body.
My parents said they knew the line would be long.
They took turns carrying my brother I walked beside them.

They say twelve hundred people filed past each hour.
They say the casket was African mahogany lined with white silk.
His face looked waxy women bent to kiss it.
His mustache was perfectly trimmed I have seen pictures.

My parents said they knew the line would be long.
The president had declared it a national day of mourning.
My brother was one and a half I was three and a half.
My brother cried my brother was hungry.

I don't know how I felt probably scared.
I don't know what I thought about the endless stricken faces.
I know they were stricken I have seen pictures.

That day riots were everywhere people were dying but not here.
That day in Washington hundreds of fires were burning.
They say it looked from the air as if the city had been bombed such
    smoke.

That day our planes were bombing North Vietnam.
And that day the bodies were rotting unburied in My Lai.
And that day King's brother gave a sermon at Ebenezer Baptist
called "Why America May Go to Hell."

That day that day they say they said.
My parents knew the line would be long.
My parents taught us there's no such thing as Hell and there isn't.
There's nowhere for America to go.

King: Apr. 7, 1968

Carmichael said it was white America that did it.
Get your gun he said some did but not here.
Hoover said he'd prevent the rise of a black messiah.
He didn't say how that was a month ago.

King said longevity has its place that was four days ago.

I have no memory of the day in question.
Closing my eyes won't bring it back pictures won't either.
I could squint like this forever what's the point.
There is no witness without memory.

My parents knew the line would be long but not this long.
My brother was crying my brother was tired and hungry.
If only he could have held out a while longer if only then what?
I wish I could say at least that we touched his sleeve.

We never even made it to the casket.

Cub Scouts of America

I laid it out myself my
                new pup-tent my
                        duty to do it
alone in that
           crisp blue uniform oh
                    where is it now
some box
        I put on my kerchief
                  snugged it to my throat
and it was I
        who gathered the tools
                who studied the rods
yes I alone
        who staked them
             who pitched gray canvas
beneath gray skies
          C.S.A.
              stenciled black on each side
My mission
       to clear the area of
            enemy snipers I
knew they'd blend in
        there in Killearn
            but I was prepared
I'd filled my grandfather's
        old canteen I'd
            loaded my Daisy
and now I raised my
       father's binoculars
            zoomed in and out
as I scouted
      our neighbors and there
           next door was Nancy

in her bedroom
                    silhouette glowing
                                        Nancy whose hair
flapped up with each step
                            whenever she stalked
                                                    away
and when I panned
                    toward my own house
                                            I saw my father
behind a window
                    blotched with azaleas
                                            staring back
Beware the enemy within
                            he sometimes intoned
                                                    weirdly
and *Wherever I go the*
                        South wounds me
                                            he wrote in a poem
and when I abandoned
                        my post for dinner
                                            my father well
he took a can of
                    silver Krylon and sprayed
                                                those letters out
I did hate him then
                        but when the sunlight
                                                hit at a slant I
could still make them
                        out those three
                                            ghosts that still haunt

Concordances: 1976

Hearing the Concorde
had been retired

brings back unbidden
an image of myself near London,

standing alone and probably depressed
outside Queen's School, at recess,

extracting from among the pence
and pocket lint in my plaid pants

(having fended off the latest inane questions
about swimming pools and "red Indians")

a brilliant uncirculated bicentennial quarter,
its muscular tricorned drummer

marching across the back,
as if into the teeth of some attack –

when suddenly overhead appeared
a marvelous metal bird,

one that could outrun,
our teacher had said, even the sun,

and which was still so close to the ground
we saw how its beak bent oddly down

toward earth, toward us, as if catching
a last glimpse of the little wingless creatures watching,

before graduating into the sheer
migratory atmosphere

of the future, bound for a place
named for the dead man on my quarter's face.

The Tallahassee of Other Days

There was no history, there were only the storms.
– Donald Justice, "The Miami of Other Days"

It was still a metropolis of trees, a mere
town of people. Longleafs and live oaks
raised their awnings over summer and winter,
over the sprawl of strip malls and the dim
suburban constellations. But the awnings
were thinning, and the canopy roads that spoked
outward toward forgotten towns – Meridian,
Bainbridge, Miccosukee – survived only
by ordinance, souvenirs of country lanes
and coaches, of the days before I-10
cleaved us like a river, and the flood of cars...

A May afternoon: I'm idling at the light
at Apalachee Parkway and Magnolia.
Around me, smug frat boys and bureaucrats
(or so I smugly guess) keeping their cool
with windows raised. Up at the intersection,
two black men sweating in three-piece suits,
extending *The Final Call;* across the road,
King Love himself, our local patron saint,
he of the long white beard, the golden crown
of paperboard, the smell that knocks you back –
he of the many placards, exhorting us
some days to love each other instead of Jesus,
some days to help him find a home and wife.
And farther on, a half-mile down the Parkway,
shifting between two capitols, new and old:
the Spanish flag, the Union Jack, Old Glory,
and the Stars and Bars... A primer of sorts.

Then south on Monroe, toward sandy washboard roads
ghosting through pinewoods, scrub, palmetto plains;
toward sinkholes tapping the veins of buried rivers –
Blue Sink, Cherokee, Big and Little Dismal:

swimming holes for drunken good ole boys
and those of us enough like them to pass;
storehouses of stolen Chevys and Clovis points,
of camel teeth and the tibias of sloths,
of the crushed shells and sands of an absent ocean.
There was nothing there that was not history.

Shades of Tucson

I have two trees in my front yard. Jesús,
our botanist neighbor, told me yesterday
I ought to cut the chinaberry down.
Non-native, he said. The other, a eucalyptus,

was planted fifty years ago by James,
who grew up in this house and who now lives
across the street, next door to Mrs. Chávez,
whose husband, James once told me, tried to drive

his family out because they were black, which
was bad enough, but worse was they had sons –
and Chávez, he had daughters. This took place
when 13th St. was dirt and the president

Eisenhower. Old Chávez died of cancer
twenty years back, and every morning now
I drink my coffee on my porch, which once
was James's porch, in eucalyptus shade,

and watch as James goes out his gate and in
the Chávez gate: he brings her paper up,
waters her plants, does little things she can't.
God ought to give him something grand for that,

or so I thought at first. But now I think
that acts like those surely repay themselves;
that every daily kindness to the widow
is a shovelful of dirt on the past's grave.

I turned from chinaberry to eucalyptus
and said: *that one's not native either, is it?*
No, said Jesús. *But this is Tucson, bro –
a person can't give up that kind of shade.*

South of Rome

The Janiculum

And at my back, a party in high gear,
a surf of noise licked by the tired salt breeze
that's sighing in from Ostia. The shy historian,

armed with a steel guitar, forgets his stutter
when he sings: *I went down to the crossroads...*
Behind us stands the wall Aurelius built,

in whose cool shade the gardener yesterday,
digging to plant a plum tree, struck a tomb.
(The archaeology fellows are still abuzz.)

Below, a taxi blurs down Via Masina,
missing a dashing cat. Above, pale stars
and a bright plane, eastbound. (Gioia del Colle?

Bosnia?) Beside me, a married abstract painter
leans on a classicist, who's pointing out
visible landmarks. Colonies of light

displace the dark. *I'm going down to Rosedale...*
I'm out of place. I'm trying to miss my wife.
The Appian ways, old and new, race south

toward the Mediterranean, toward Velletri,
the ancient hill town (maps in my head like flares,
like telescopes) on whose dark slopes my grandfather,

the day before Rome fell, was killed – his first
day of combat. And I have made it to Rome.
Someone hands me another cup of wine.

Nettuno Beach

We park in a seedy lot, then pick our way,
Anzio at our backs across the bay,
south over iron-black sand, past games of soccer,

sprawled bodies, and a shattered concrete bunker
left there like litter. Farther south, beyond
these crowds, stragglers scoop clay from a lip of land

that falls six feet or so, from grass to sand,
and coat themselves; as the gray dries, it turns
a marbly white (one woman, clad only in clay,

strikes Venus poses at the water's edge;
a man snaps photos). On we walk, beyond
a warning sign: we've entered army land,

this stretch of beach a firing range in winter –
but winter's over, so the beach is ours.
(The only other people near: an old

gay couple, holding hands, still farther south.
By whom are we afraid to be observed?)
We lay our blanket amid the sea's refusals:

mineral-water bottles, orphaned shoes,
old nets, a plastic fifty-gallon drum,
made in Japan. But there are treasures too,

and my friend has an eye: chunks of mosaic tiles
from ancient villas that used to line this coast;
smooth shards of blue *pasta di vetro*; and two

species of marble – deep red *porfido*,
green *serpentino* – whose quarries long ago
gave out. The only marble I find dates,

my friend says, from *the empire of the sixties*.
And these odd things that look like plastic? *Ossi
di seppia…* And so Montale comes to me

with his old mantra, insisting, like the sea,
on what we're not, what we do not desire.
Anzio shimmers. The sea hangs from its wire.

The Sicily Rome Cemetery

The plush grass stretches over the curved earth.
The bone-white crosses and stars of David blur
into stripes. Beyond them, rows of cypress trees:

bored sentries backed by blue. I prop carnations
(cheapest of flowers) against the cross I've come for –
my little travesty of resurrection –

and sit a while as if waiting for a judge.
I pluck the grass the mower missed. I trace
his recessed name, his rank and date, recalling

a photo: his tick-eradication bill
(he won great praise for that) has just been signed;
he's shaking hands with Governor Allred, beaming –

folks said he'd soon be governor himself…
But then he left his wife and a little girl –
my aging mother – for an Austin woman,

which cost him reelection. So what then?
Too old for any draft, he volunteered.
His final letter to my mother came,

ghost-like, after this cable: *Ragsdale led*
a patrol to clear the area of enemy snipers…
three snipers were killed… Ragsdale rushed another,

firing his carbine… was shot… And then the part
about how brave he'd been. Is that what he was?
It looks to me as though he ran away.

And yet I come back every year or so,
to sit alone, amid the marble crowd,
and argue with a man I ought to know.

The Velletri Grape Festival

He's coming right at me, through the thronged
medieval main street of this bombed-out
and rebuilt hill town, perched above the heads

of the earthbound, each of us with our plastic cup
of new wine, above children with their grape-bunch
balloons – coming right at me, looking down

from high on his unicycle, his eyes seeming to say
that his presence here can be ignored only
at my peril, and at his too, that he may fall

from that height, that I may be too close or slow,
and I freeze, no idea which way to turn,
no one to snatch me aside, but the near-falls

seem almost rehearsed, so that we're meant,
I finally guess, to doubt him, so that only children,
who shrink toward parents or point, eyes wide,

from a safe remove, really believe he'll fall, which
he doesn't, not now: he careens smoothly around me
and keeps on faltering his slow way through us.

SECOND SKINS

Keopuolani Eats a Banana: 1819

Such food was always you must remember
taboo for women – penalty of death.
Taboo also to eat in the presence of men.
Penalty also of death.
                    I bade my smallest son
sit down with me, as we had seen the white men
sit with their women. I bade him show me how
to pull the yellow skin from the white fruit,

and it was there – in the child's presence,
and in the presence also of my eldest son,
the new king, who watched us then with
all the eyes he had,
                    and in the presence also
you must remember of our old gods –
that I put that fruit in my own mouth and ate.
I lived, and the tide brought the Reverend

Bingham and his Christ, who arrived to find
our old gods strewn like speechless whales
(penalty of death!) on the strange new
beach of my tongue.

Mr. Cook's Day: Feb. 14, 1835

I have consumed the letters and accounts
so often, and have lain so many nights
in doldrums of insomnolence, waiting
for sleepwinds, that my husband's final voyage
has passed through tales and knowledge
into the dream-fogged realm of memory,
displacing that realm's natives: the Gray boy
who kissed me once before consumption took him –
vivid since childhood, he's nothing now but gray;
my first three children, who as children died;
and mother and her harsh admonishments,

grown almost kind. Such lives
concerned mine once, though some days I believe
I burst full-grown from my husband's tricorned head,
bearing his memories, which live on in me.
The kettle boiling over the fire now
is less real, as will be the taste of the tea –
the only taste I will today allow.
Today as I have done four days each year
(one day for Mr. Cook, one for each son
who lived to die a man) I shut me in
to fast, to feast on them, on memories

and dreams: blue waters blurring bluer air.
A mainsail notches both like the thin moon
of his fingernail as it traced his routes for me
upon this very map, a map whose marks
are there because he was.
I am the seer and the seen: the island,
still undiscovered, aching to be known;
the man with one eye closed and a glass trained
on feathered hills, chafed shores,
stiff palms that wave like wives at navy docks.
I never have and never shall leave England,

yet I have been, in sleep or waking visions,
transported. Often I'm the island girl
cutting through breakers in the long canoe
between two men, an infant in my arms,
my grass skirts flowing in the salty breeze,
the floating forest rising up before us –
even the shorebirds come to scrutinize
these leafless trees, this strange arboreal race
of men – where have their women gone? their children?
And why so ghostly and so ravenous?
They might have just escaped some blighted land,

yet they are rich: they have loose second skins
fitted with doors from which unearthly treasures
emerge at intervals. Until they came
we never had felt poor; they taught us that.
They taught us many new economies.
The only girl on deck, I bear the gaze
of their whole race. And Mr. Cook looks too,
but does not, cannot, know me.
I see him doubly: he's my husband, his child
it is that sucks at me, and yet he stands
a stranger also, a man of unknown race

and godlike ways – surely he is a god.
We treat him as though he were, and all his men:
they carry fire between their lips and sticks
that spit forth bolts of thunder in their hands.
We slaughter hundreds of our fattest hogs,
a season's worth and more,
whatever we have we give them and they take.
Our women, too, we give them and they take.
Sometimes I'm sitting in a palm's thatched shade
with a pale god whose eyes are animal,
and he begins by giving me a nail,

and as I hold it to the light and bite it
his mouth descends on me as he unlaces
his stinking breeches, till I see his parts
monstrous before me, jeweled
with sores and blisters. When I try to shriek
no sound comes out, but always there's the cleaver
I'd stolen from the ship: I slash awake,
my nightclothes wet, as if I'd caught his fever,
the chambermaid regarding me with fright.
(She soothes me back to sleep with a sweet song –
tell me the tales that to me were so dear...)

Or else I'm offered for Mr. Cook's delight,
but always he rejects the gift of me,
kindly though firmly. If I blush with shame
it's not for having been so offered, but
for having so desired he take me. Once
this changed: he took me to his hut, my heart
a luffed sail rattling, and we sat on mats
as the sea sang outside through trees and wind,
sang softly in the lustered dark, and I
was young again and looked as once I did
but browner, like a nut, and next to mine

his leathered skin was pale,
so pale! Instead of lying with me then,
he questioned me about our lives and ways
until we slept. When I awoke, his ship
was gone. The bay was utterly bereft.
When I awoke again, back to this life,
the nearest water was the dirty Thames…
I have outlived my husband by fifty years,
and all my ill-starred progeny combined.
I wait for my own time, which doesn't come,
though I at least grow less and less myself

and more the islander, trapped in this skin,
this sunless world – like Mr. Cook's Omai,
who mastered chess and was the toast of London,
or Bougainville's Ahutoru, who grew to love
even Parisian opera. Natives here
are pale as ghosts and never would survive
(it seems to me as I observe their ways)
without their second skins and thunder sticks –
the relics, I surmise,
of some exploring god, baubles he gave them
in trade for their ancestral paradise.

Such gifts, though useful here, may fail to save them.

Family History: Oct. 15, 1848

The instruments were various:
the hollow pens that spilled their inks
on pale, absorbent fields of paper;
the notion that land belongs to men;
apologetic rhetoric
("the force of circumstance" and "hard
necessity"); the trade in rum
and viruses; and guns, of course;

and love: in Texas, a decade after
New Echota and the Trail of Tears,
an Alabama Cherokee
with rivers of hair and broken eyes
married a white man. He was disowned;
she fell into the pool of us and drowned.

Overland Wedding: May 21, 1850

Such a shivaree we gave them that night.
By the time I'd found a husband of my own
seven months later, we had no such foolery
left in us, nothing but dumb astonishment.
Yet I am blessed to be alive, even here
in Nevada City, where my Jason gazes
at the far hills and the green valley, praising
the "beauty uncivilized" of California,
a metal gleam in the brown pools of his eyes.
The only woman here, I mostly see
mouths – my children's and the miners' – open
in my mind's eye like baby birds', and none
but me to fill them.
                    Such a shivaree…
It was early in the passage: half a year,
nearly, before we rode, pinching our nostrils,
through the last carcass field – wagons abandoned
beside the parched, starved hulks that had hauled them
as far as they were able; months before
we passed the Dutchman prodding his overbrimming
wheelbarrow westward through the desert heat,
his bare hands redder than any Indian's;
before we scratched our names with charred stick-ends
on Independence Rock, or traded hard bread
for soft Sioux moccasins; before the hail
battered us or the bloody flux slowed us
or cholera winnowed us; weeks before
the plains to the far horizon blackened and smoldered
with buffalo; before we ate buffalo steak
or tongue, or baked buffalo marrow in coals
of buffalo chips; before I learned to shoot,
in case the savages, who more than once
would save us from ourselves, turned savage;
and one week to the day before we found
the fresh grave, still preserved by rough-hewn pickets

against the wolves, of Isaac Davis, a schoolmate,
whose clear voice, when he sang, would carry through
the still Wisconsin evenings to our porch,
a splendid voice...
                    Such a shivaree –
enough, I thought, to rouse the Seven Sleepers.
The couple, after their vows, climbed in a wagon,
men tugged the tongue, we shouldered from behind,
rolling them, all of us laughing, half a mile
into the prairie. We blew flutes and fiddled,
banged cans and shot revolvers till midnight,
then left them there alone with just the sound
of God's breath rushing through the bowing grasses.
Well after dawn, they shambled into camp,
smiling and shy, to a charmed ruckus of cheers.
The sugared hope that fattened our spirits then
would prove, for some of us, enough to live on.

The Origin of Chinese Laundry in America: 1851

Laundresses being scarce in the gold camps,
the richest forty-niners shipped soiled clumps

of clothes as far as – this is true – Hong Kong.
They came back clean and pressed, and before long

men rode the laundry's scented slipstream east,
their old world melting into Chinese mist

as they chased news they couldn't not believe
across the Pacific, toward the leaking hive

of California – Guangdong credit sharks
behind them; foreigner taxes, burnt-out shacks,

and their black queues hacked off ahead. One man,
Wah Lee, forced from the fields he'd come to mine,

opened a laundry at Washington and Grant
and made himself a San Francisco mint.

Cowboys and Indians: 1882

1. Spring

Folks say that if they owned both Hell and Texas
they'd dwell in the cooler place and rent out Texas.
But I arrived in February, cold,
and come March I was swimming the Rio Grande
into the belly of America, shivering
in underclothes, astride ole Nigger Boy,

my favorite mount, as strong as he was black,
and so big-barreled that he swam like a duck.
We were a dozen men, a hundred horses,
and several thousand head of long-legged cattle
bound for the Blackfoot Lands in North Montana.
"You can thank me for having jobs," said Reb

one night as we played cards around the fire.
"After the late unpleasantness, I headed
west from Georgia, and I myself reduced
the nation's herd of buffalo by half.
And it was Frank, my partner, killed the rest."
"I ought to whup your ass if you're to thank,"

Quarternight said. "I rubbed tobacco juice
in my eyes again today to stay awake –
three times." "Why ain't you sleeping now?" Reb asked.
"Well, a man needs a little conversation,
is what I reckon. A little liquor, too.
And cards, a course. I'll get some sleep come winter."

2. Summer

By day, we might be fording rivers, or else
trying to keep the parched herd, every tongue
slung out, from balking, milling, turning back
toward the last water, going blind with thirst…
One morning early we crested a hill to find
a virgin valley, an Eden, no sign of man,

only the ghost of a great buffalo trail
wisping away like smoke. That day we spied
a cow and calf – Reb must've missed a couple –
and the veal we ate that night was a rare treat.
And other days, herd-brained stampedes, or rustlers.
Women and fights in Dodge and Ogalalla.

And Indians too – one day a motley band
tried to insist we pay a ten-beeve toll
for passing through their lands. Their old chief dwelt
on the fact that he had always, against others,
counseled peace with the white man. Our foreman
proved a slicker diplomat, denying

his right to a toll, but offering two beeves
as a token of goodwill, since they looked hungry.
And he explained how all the rest were gifts
from the chief of white men to another tribe
that welcomed our priests and teachers. Which was true.
Which gave them pause. We left them with that thought.

3. Fall

Snow had fallen already, and I wondered
how southern herds would last through such a winter.
Our coming had been ballyhooed for weeks,
and our approach delighted every Blackfoot –
they flocked to the Agency from nearby villages,
all gaudily bedecked, fine specimens

of aborigines. Though they were spirited,
we were by then – man, horse, and cow – worn down.
(I'm fool enough to do the drive again,
but after half a year the charm had gone.
I think I'd rather be the Indian,
sit with a pretty squaw and smoke a pipe,

and let some other fellow drive the cows
to me – there'd be a heap more comfort in it.)
When the time came to go our separate ways,
I knew I'd miss a few of my fellow drivers
but never guessed how keenly I would feel,
that late September evening in Montana,

the parting between myself and Nigger Boy.
A horse and rider share the trail's hardships,
and an affection grows that's nearly human.
A man's not lonely with a horse like that.
His bones may lie now bleaching in some coulee,
but I who knew him never shall forget him.

Two Moon to a Journalist after Rehearsal: 1898

I thought then that the Great Spirits
had made the Sioux, put them there,
and white men and the Cheyenne here,
expecting fights. The Great Spirits,
I thought, liked fighting – it was to them
like play. So I joined Crazy Horse,
and at the place called Little Big Horn
we wiped the white men from the earth.

Shooting was quick – pop, pop, pop.
Soldiers dropped, horses fell on them.
One white man I remember rode
a sorrel mare, back and forth,
shouting and waving. He was brave,
I do not know his name. The bugler
kept blowing his commands, brave too.
A white chief, maybe Long Hair, fell.

Then one bunch of white men was left.
Then one man all alone ran far,
down toward the river, up a hill.
I thought he'd live, but a young Sioux
shot him in the back of the head.
We stripped the bodies, so to keep them
from fighting again in the next life.
And that night we were still with sorrow.

It was a great fight, smoke and dust.
But that was twenty years ago,
and old minds change. I do not know
what the Great Spirits want today.
I do know what your people want –
the show business, the Wild West Show.
Tomorrow Long Hair's widow comes,
and we will play the fight again.

Coin of the Realm: 1913

Heads: Iron Tail

This face is not Big Tree.
This face is not Two Moon.
They also posed for him,
yes, but look: the face
on the nickel is mine. Meant
to portray a race, of course,

not a particular man.
A symbol's what they want.
Sign of the savage place
they civilized. Of course.
But look: this coin, this face
in front of you. You see?

Tails: Black Diamond

Cement and iron. Cement
and men. And the great weight,
great as the skies close
and drift, everything drifting,
gates becoming plains
endless as open skies,

and the sweetgrass, the sweetgrass
and the body of the One
as far as the skies can see –
a bark, and the gates again,
and the face of the human one,
and gray cement, and iron.

HOMELAND SECURITY

The Nights

The screamer sleeps, inside.
The desert's wide awake:
the mouse, the rattlesnake.
I've come out here to hide,

behind our house, below
the riddled sky, afraid
of what our bodies made.
To the south: Mexico...

These are the nights men run.
Guaymas before midday,
a beach-town life... I play
it out. Such things are done.

The Rincons seep like a stain
into the paling east.
The borders are policed.
The wail, nearby, of a train.

Laiku

Culture is nature.
It isn't a disaster.
There's no need to look.

We do not torture
We did not trade weapons for –
I am *not* a crook.

Lauds

My eyes open to a cry,
then flinch back shut. O Lord make haste to help me.
Why can't he wake up like the saints,

joyful in glory? Let him sing aloud
in his crib (but softly) one of those
damn lullabies we always –

O harden not your heart!
I feel it too: the urge to wake up screaming.
Beneath the harps, beneath the timbrels,

a nightmare noise: the chuckle of iron fetters,
the snicker of our two-edged swords
executing vengeance

upon the heathen – hear it?
God's praise like gristle in the swordsmen's mouths.
And thou, child, shalt be called the prophet –

what's this now? silence? Let Israel rejoice!
And let thy father, who is still
in bed, sleep a bit longer…

And forgive him. And praise
your screaming brethren, and not just those of Zion,
for Christ's sake, for crying out loud.

The Mystery of the Barbarity of Charles Graner

"Let's get this straight: Charles Graner
is not America. America would never
hold a knife to his wife's throat, then say
when she woke that he was considering
killing her. And America's wife in turn
would never call her husband "my own
Hannibal Lecter." Am I right, or what?
Charles Graner may be Hannibal Lecter,
but he is not America. America is not that
kind of husband. Nor would America email
his adolescent children photos of himself
torturing naked Iraqi prisoners and say
"look what Daddy gets to do!" Am I right?
America is not that kind of father. America
would never torture naked Iraqi prisoners.
Let's be absolutely clear about all of this.
And America's ex-lover and co-defendant
would never whisper to the sketch artist
at America's trial: "You forgot the horns."
Charles Graner may or may not have horns,
but America is horn-free. America does not
torture prisoners. America may render them,
fully clothed, to Egypt or Syria, for further
interrogation, or to men like Charles Graner,
but America is not, *ipso facto*, Egypt or Syria,
and Charles Graner is not now nor has he ever
been America. And don't talk to me about
Guantanamo. Please! Let's get this straight.
You and I know who America is. We know
what America does and doesn't do, because we
(not Charles Graner!) are America. Am I right?
Is this all clear? Tell me – am I right, or what?"

Homeland Security

The four a.m. cries
of my son worm
through the double
foam of earplugs

and diazepam.
The smoke alarm's
green eye glows.
Beneath the cries,

the squirm and bristle
of the night's catch
of fiddlebacks
on the glue-traps

guarding our bed.
Necrotic music.
Scored in my head.
And all night columns

of ants have tramped
through the ruins
of my sleep, bearing
the fipronil

I left for them
home to their queen.
Patriot ants.
Out of republics

endlessly perishing.
If I can hold
out long enough,
maybe my wife

will go. If she
waits long enough,
maybe he'll go back
down on his own.

Dispatches from the Interior

Like the one where you stumble along happily drunk after closing a bar and reach your car only to find it surrounded by militia who take you in to question you about why you left your son alone in the car so long and you say I lost track of time though that's not true and Can I see him and they refuse and Is he okay and you're panicking and thinking What if he died in there or the one the very next night when you find yourself atop some posh hotel listening to some poet speaking and realize you haven't seen your son since morning when you let him go down to the lobby alone to play despite the warnings you now recall about the natives and you race for the elevator but there is no elevator and so you find the stairs and descend floor by floor and each landing is a shabby apartment living room and though you can sometimes tell someone is home water running for instance or light under a shut door you never see an actual person or gain any insight into this country of ancient dearth and modern resentment what country is this anyway? and after the gauntlet of these empty private foreign lives you emerge at last into a brightly lit and darkly paneled colonial lobby and scramble frantic now through the patrician crowd looking for help but when you ask the giant suited man if he speaks English he replies in the plummiest nasals I don't just speak it I am it and merely cocks a brow about your son so you race outside where a boy squats alone in the penumbra by a bush and you tilt his face to the light but he isn't yours too small too dark and you keep looking and see others and scream one name and then oh god you see his hunched familiar shape rise out of the pile of dead leaves he had hidden under and falter toward you arms outstretched the pajamas he was wearing this morning now tattered and filthy and when you scoop him up you discover obscenities and anti-American slogans scrawled on his forehead and cheeks and blood or something caking his nostrils and he doesn't speak or cry and nothing shines forth from those eyes and you carry him cradle him through this endless third-world night trying to comfort him but knowing you'll never be able to comfort him but cooing You're safe now Daddy is here or the one

From *The Zekiad*

The girl had been raised to ripeness in a crib.
Now she was wrapped in something like a burqa
(or maybe just a hoodie and long skirt)

and trussed up in the bed of a Chevy truck.
Our hero drove, horny for God and murder,
until he came, at last, to The Loud Red Room,

which was more loud than red. He gave a snort
like a starved laugh and cleared the room of patrons
by flashing them his best Guantanamo smile,

the one that said that he'd be squeezing limes
in their clamped-open eyes should they remain.
Only the barkeep stayed behind. His name,

according to his name tag, was Kamal,
and though the name was fake, he was Islamic,
exiled of old from his dream of Palestine,

where he still spent his Technicolor nights,
to this blue-state backwater. He wore a locket,
and out our hero reached, as if to tickle

it open, then swerved to drop the Chevy keys
in his shirt pocket, shouting *These are for Zeke!*
over the deafening blare. *Here comes the judge!*

the barkeep seemed to answer. And the judge
did enter then, a kidskin-covered sap
in one hand and a double-barrel of whup-ass

in the other, with a toddler's air of authority.
A toddler who, when there's food, is a big eater.

Trip Hop

I'll pack my toothbrush
and my cyanide molar
the iPhone the car-seats
and a tactical stroller

I'll pack a snack-bag
with the Kraft food groups
and white flags for me
and black for my troops

I'll pack a fresh pack
of Shark double-edge blades
my boy's Razor scooter
and my girl's blue shades

I'll pack doses of patience
and some Kevlar smiles
check our air and our fluids
our gauges and dials

and we'll hit I-40
in our old green Accord
there'll be collateral damage
and we might get bored

but I won't need TomTom
to know where I'm headed
a theme park they dream of
a theme park I've dreaded

and if we ever get home
and if our home still stands
I'll unpack my dark heart
and Purell my hands

Under the New Regime

In the main square an empty plinth
    on which wild children play.
Only their parents recall the god
    and how he got carried away.

One Morning

The boy is wide awake:
he climbs into our bed
and clambers toward my head,
wielding a yellow rake.

Combing my hair, the boy
giggles with every stroke.
His is a simple joke:
he knows his plastic toy

is not a comb, my hair
is not disheveled sand,
and yet his furrowed mind
has seen a likeness there –

delight grows from small seeds.
And for now I won't worry
what else might, as we hurry
toward what the future breeds.

AMERICAN ORNITHOLOGY

Wilson and the Ivory-Bill: 1808

The bird from which this likeness has been made
   was wounded only slightly in the wing.
      His voice recalled exactly the violent cries
   of a child in pain – endless panicked shrieking
that terrified my horse. Our shrill parade
      through Wilmington elicited surprise:
      windows filled with faces, which filled with eyes.

I was received at the inn with real alarm,
   by females especially. When I declared
      I sought a room for myself and my small child
   (I played it well), how foolishly they stared!
Drawing the bundle from beneath my arm,
      I showed the livid bird: his screams, though wild,
      were drowned by the mirth of those I had beguiled.

I locked him in my room to tend my horse.
   When I returned, plaster covered the floor
      beneath his perch above the window, where
   a great hole gaped in the lath. An hour more,
the weatherboards would have yielded to his force
      and he might still be plying that Southern air –
      his image lost to us, but restored there.

I felt the failure mine as I watched him die,
   though it was he who refused all proffered food.
      Once, when he cut me as I took his drawing,
   I rendered his bright crest with my fresh blood,
briefly conveying his nobility –
      before it browned, it was a splendid thing.
      He was but slightly wounded in the wing.

Wilson and the Carolina Parakeet: 1810

Dear Bartram,
                    I enclose a recent sketch,
a paroquet obtained near Big Bone lick.
Her flock alighted on a sycamore,
thronging its winter branches like summer leaves.
Though each successive discharge of my gun
brought showers down, their sympathy was such
that after a looping circuit through the air
they settled again above their prostrate brethren.
The tree releafed!
                    The specimen you see
was wounded only slightly in the wing:
soon she was husking seeds from cockle-burs
and gnawing at the bars of her stick-cage.
Perched in the stern, she piloted our vessel
down the Ohio (past one sylvan scholar
who thought its name – *The Ornithologist* –
derived from the Iroquois!) to Louisville.

Science and literature are friendless there;
I found not one subscriber, only a damned
bedizened Frenchman, known as Oh-Doo-Bon,
who smirked a little when he saw my drawings
and hemmed and hawed in Froggish with his damned
bedizened friend. *Might he subscribe?* I asked.
Ah no, monsieur. And worse, he showed his drawings –
which were, it pains me to confess, quite good.

On leaving there, I snugged the bird in silk
and, now on horseback, carried her in my pocket,
unbinding her for meals, which she devoured.
In recommitting her to "durance vile"
we often quarreled – she thus, and more than once,
paid me in kind for the wound I'd given her.
Twice she escaped in the deepest wilderness;

twice I was tempted to emancipate her –
but each time I pursued.
                              I carried her
a thousand miles. We crossed the Chickasaw
and Choctaw nations, where I forged, through Polly,
many a bond. At Natchez, Dunbar gave her
a proper cage; I hung it out of doors
where passing flocks were drawn to Polly's call:
several parties in trees conversed at length
with my gregarious prisoner.
                              One such suitor
I wounded slightly in the wing. That night
the fond pair nestled together, Polly's head
tucked underneath the plumage of her mate.
Ah, she was heartsick when he died! But then,
in New Orleans, I bought a looking-glass,
and all her former fondness seemed to return:
she burbled to the glass and dozed against it.

By now she knew her name and came when called;
she perched upon my shoulders, ate from my mouth,
learned more of Scottish than the English know…
Determined to continue her instruction,
I brought her with me when I went to sea –
would I had not! One morning as I slept
she freed herself and perished in the Gulf.

The figure in this sketch – my sole companion
many a lonesome day – is a faithful likeness.

Audubon and the Passenger Pigeon: 1831

Let us now, kind reader, inspect their roosting-place
along the banks of the Green River. When I arrived,
few pigeons could be seen, but of the human race
there was no shortage. Nor of horses, wagons, guns.
(Nor hogs: three hundred had been driven ninety miles

to fatten themselves on birdflesh.) Carpets of white dung
lay thick beneath prodigious maples, ancient oaks.
The damage to those trees – massive branches broken,
trunks snapped – resembled a tornado's aftermath.
Such signs implied a flock immense beyond conception;

still I was unprepared for what I soon would witness.
Men waited, many with torches, poles, or pots of sulphur,
the rest with guns. The sun had set before we heard them.
Their din, even at distance, was like a gale at sea –
indeed I felt a wind as they passed over us.

Thousands were knocked to earth by poles, but still they lit,
one perching on another till limbs began at last
to shatter. Useless it was to speak, useless to shout
to one's companion. Even the mouths of guns seemed mute,
although the pantomime of firing and reloading

did not abate till dawn approached. By then, the flock
was ready to move on, and all that could fly soon
had flown. Then only did the authors of that slaughter
enter amongst the dead and dying, loading their wagons
as high as they could be heaped, then letting loose the hogs.

Hearing this tale, dear reader, you may fear for pigeons.
But years have passed since these events, which are replayed
routinely, and still the flocks are unreduced in size.
Indeed my studies have persuaded me that nothing,
save loss of our great forests, could lead to their demise.

Audubon and the Golden Eagle: 1833

I should confess that, as I watched his eye
and caught its air of proud disdain,
I felt two instincts vie –
let me explain,
or try:
first, I
desired to free
that creature, let him fly,
wings spread again, away from me,
back to the rock-tipped regions of the sky –

yet though I knew how noble that would be,
I paused, dear reader, when I heard
a voice, a whispered plea:
That splendid bird!
Oh, we
would see
that splendid bird!
Therefore, most dutifully,
as though I'd given you my word,
I took his life – which nearly finished me:

I draped his cage, set smoking coals beneath,
and sealed him in, thus to be gassed.
I prayed for his quick death.
But *two days* passed.
At last,
I thrust
steel through his chest,
which brought us both relief.
This drawing stands amongst my best
but left me broken, ill, speechless with grief.

HEADLANDS

Confluence

Here on this tongue of land
     that laps the place where the St. Mark's
and the Wakulla come together,
     on grounds haunted by a thousand years
of the middens and the mounds
     of the Apalachee, here, where Spaniards
built a fort they called San Marcos,
     first of wood (burned down), again of wood
(blown down), then at last of stone,
     which passed to England, then back to Spain,
from whom Jackson snatched it,
     and of which only the foundations remain –
here, as I have been trying to say,
     upon these layered grounds, upon this
speechless tongue, here upon land
     that was everyone else's before and after
it was ours, the woman I loved and I
     came down to the water's edge at dusk,
as thirsting animals will, a woman
     later looked for in other women, and in myself,
and we were the latest triumphant army,
     we ruled the conquered dead awhile, voices
bright flags rippling from our throats,
     bodies twin rivers spilling together toward
the Gulf, rivers from whose brackish
     currents we may never stop drinking.

A Hike in the Headlands

We can't shake it, this flightless bird
that emerged from the murk to shadow us
like a sheepdog. It nips at our thighs,
to herd us together, perhaps, or to keep us
awake, or to steer us shrewdly away
from some nest that lies shrouded now
in this milky mist. How can we know?
There are known unknowns and –
how does it go? Sometimes it flaps its wings,
cocks a wide red eye at you, at me.
The stings from its beak gentle pangs
that bloom on the skin, then sink in
like a sigh. Or else it simply found itself,
as we had hoped to do, alone, the last
of its ilk – if so, we should surely record
its song for posterity, ferry its tones into
the creature-poor future, like Chinese monks
smuggling the secret of silk into Europe.
It has been following us now all day,
fat and fearless, like those stupid birds
explorers of old slaughtered whole hosts of,
salting them, filling the holds of their ships.
Their names now ghosts that haunt us, words
to conjure absence by. Perhaps it grew fat
on human food and wants more, from us.
But look – we have no human food! And we
ourselves are lean. It puffs its chest and preens,
it screaks out a tune, it waves those useless
wings again. Hello? Goodbye? Surprising
little eddies of air. Kill-me salt-me eat-me –
is that it? How can we know? We do not trust
ourselves to know. Goodbye! Hello!
There are known unknowns and unknown
unknowns – that's what it was. And that much
we too can say. We keep walking into the mist,

hand in warm hand, that minimal touch –
into the swirling eggwhite mist, not knowing
whether it's following us or leading the way.

Portage

I carried the canoe above my head.
I heard the water, the birdsong, the wind,
I heard the reptiles, as I passed, dropping
from branches into water. But I saw
only the path at my feet, skinned with leaves,
veined with thick roots. My muscles burned, my mind
fogged over, and I thought, time and again,
of giving up – of cutting to the bank
and gliding, easy, back to camp, the way
my broken oar had glided off that morning,

but something like a thirst kept pushing me,
some unwilled willfulness I can't account for,
can take no credit for, till the air cooled,
till light began to yellow and the path
frayed to an end at last beside the thing
I'd come here for: the unspoiled source of waters
I'd long known only muddied versions of
but now, as Bartram had, saw running clear.
I dropped the boat, stripped off my sweaty clothes,
and leapt into that clarity with a shout

to scare the ghosts and gators. Down I swam
against the force of all that rising water,
chasing a school of bream, a brace of turtles,
learning the coolness of the underworld,
before returning to the air, renewed.
I put my open mouth to the river's surface
and drank it in – as if to clarify
myself. But weariness was filling me,
like crickets filling the space between the trees,
and so I launched my boat, scraping the sand,

slipping past cypress knees into the current.
Now I can see the land I struggled through:
was that the point – the blind, exhausting portage?
Or was it the brief idyll at the springs?
Or this – this retrospective drifting back?
The river twins each image but its own,
and soon the world recedes until it's nothing
but rows of leaning trees and double skies.
I mustn't sleep, I think, closing my eyes,
as what I once had carried carries me.

Notes

"Angela's Passage"

> My image of Angela was derived from Linda M. Heywood and John K. Thornton's description of her in *Central Africans, Atlantic Creoles, and the Foundation of the Americas, 1585-1660* (2007).

"Wheatley in the Tower of London"

> When Wheatley (1753–1784), still a slave, traveled to London in the summer of 1773 for the launch of her *Poems*, the first book in English by an African, she became "the most famous African on the face of the earth" (Henry Louis Gates, *The Trials of Phillis Wheatley*). In a letter written after she was freed, she described her visit to the Tower of London with the English abolitionist Granville Sharp, and it was Vincent Carretta's speculation about this visit, in his introduction to Wheatley's *Complete Writings*, that sparked my own. In the same letter, she described matter-of-factly the economic challenges that faced her as a writer now that she was "upon her own footing." But with war looming, publishers were printing less poetry in general, and Wheatley was in a particularly tough spot: her publisher and much of her audience were in England, but her work was pro-independence (her poem to the Earl of Dartmouth, for example, links her own desire for freedom from bondage to America's desire for freedom from England). Unable to obtain enough advance subscriptions to publish her next book, she died indigent and was buried in an unmarked grave. As Gates puts it, "Wheatley's freedom had enslaved her to a life of hardship."

"The State of Virginia"

> This poem was inspired by (and loosely quotes from) a letter from a white Virginian to an acquaintance in Cincinnati (whom I tchanged into a sister). The letter originally appeared in the Cincinnati *Journal* and was later quoted in the Jan. 28, 1832, issue of William Lloyd Garrison's new abolitionist weekly, *The Liberator*. I first came across it in Herbert Aptheker's *American Negro Slave Revolts* (1943).

"Day of Settlement"

> John Brown, Jr. (1821–1895), eldest son of John Brown (1800–1859), detailed his father's system of corporal punishment in letters to F.B. Sanborn, editor of *The Life and Letters of John Brown: Liberator of Kansas, and Martyr of Virginia* (1885). Robert E. Lee, then a Marine colonel, commanded the company that captured Brown.

"Whitman on Broadway"

Whitman (1819–1892) describes the moment he first heard news of the attack on Ford Sumter in the "Opening of the Secession War" section of his *Specimen Days in America* (1887).

"William Howard Russell at Bull Run"

Russell (1820–1907), an Irish journalist, was the first modern war correspondent, and his controversial account of Bull Run appeared in *The Times* of London and later in volume two of *My Diary North and South* (1863). I first encountered it in *The Civil War: The First Year Told By Those Who Lived It* (2011), a Library of America anthology edited by Brooks D. Simpson, Stephen W. Sears, and Aaron Sheehan-Dean. I learned of the sesquicentennial reenactment from a *Washington Post* article, "Thousands Watch, and Sweat, as Battle of Bull Run Is Fought Again" (July 23, 2011), by Michael E. Ruane and June Q. Wu.

"Frank Haskell at Gettysburg"

This poem draws on the classic account given by Frank Haskell (1828–1864) to his brother and published posthumously. (Haskell was killed at the Battle of Cold Harbor.)

"James Daniel Brock at Cold Harbor"

This poem takes details from *Campaigning with Grant* (1907), by Horace Porter, and *The Civil War: An Illustrated History*, by Geoffrey C. Ward, with Ric Burns and Ken Burns (1990).

"Monroe's Doctrine"

I've conflated two anecdotes from the diaries of Mary Boykin Chesnut (1823–1886). In one, Chesnut recounts a tale about a neighbor's slave, named Monroe, who advises his mistress (also named Mary) about the perils of impudence. In the other, one of Chesnut's own slaves, having kept Chesnut's diamonds safe from Union soldiers, returns them as if they were "garden peas." (*Mary Chesnut's Civil War*, C. Vann Woodward, ed.,1981.)

"Grant on His Deathbed"

The details here are adapted from the memoirs of U. S. Grant (1822–1885). This poem is in memory of the poet Rachel Wetzsteon (1967–2009), whose book *Sakura Park* (which features Grant's tomb on the cover) drew me to that place shortly after she had left it.

Notes

Concordances

"Seeing Armstrong"

This poem is based on Charles Black's essay, "My World with Louis Armstrong" (*The Yale Review*, Fall 1979).

"The Tallahassee of Other Days"

This poem is in memory of Kamal Abou Youssef (1933–1999), better known in Tallahassee as King Love.

Second Skins

"Keopuolani Eats a Banana"

Keopuolani (1778?–1823) was the highest-ranking wife of King Kamehameha 1, whose death in 1819 led to the '*Ai noa* (literally "free eating"), a period of taboo-breaking that culminated in the renunciation of the ancient Hawaiian code known as the *kapu*. Christian missionaries, led by Hiram Bingham, arrived a few months later. My sources included Sheldon Dibble's *History of the Sandwich Islands* (1843) and Mary Charlotte Alexander's *The Story of Hawaii* (1912).

"Mr. Cook's Day"

The speaker is Elizabeth Cook (1742–1835), widow of Captain James Cook (1728–1779), the first European to land on the Hawaiian Islands. Details in the poem are taken from *The Explorations of Captain James Cook in the Pacific: As Told by Selections of His Own Journals, 1768–1779*, edited by Sir Archibald Grenfell Price (1957).

"Family History"

The parenthetical quotations (which I found in Howard Zinn's *A People's History of the United States*) are from Sen. Edward Everett's explanation of his decision, in 1836, to vote to ratify the Treaty of New Echota, which authorized the forcible relocation of the Cherokee Nation from the southeast to present-day Oklahoma.

"Overland Wedding"

Many of the details in this poem were taken from *Women's Diaries of the Westward Journey,* edited by Lillian Schlissel. My speaker is a composite of several of the real-life women who speak in those pages.

"The Origin of Chinese Laundry in America"

I found Wah Lee in Geoffrey Ward's *The West* (1996).

"Cowboys and Indians"
>This poem is a distillation of *The Log of a Cowboy: A Narrative of the Old Trail Days* (1903), a novel by Andy Adams (1859–1935), based on his years riding the Great Western Cattle Trail.

"Two Moon to a Journalist after Rehearsal"
>*McClure's Magazine* (Sept. 1898) ran an account of the Battle of Little Big Horn by a Cheyenne chief, Two Moon (1847–1917). I took details from that piece but invented Two Moon's role in the popular reenactment that toured as part of Buffalo Bill's Wild West Show. Yet it's not far-fetched: some veterans of the battle did participate in the reenactment, and Sitting Bull himself toured with the Show for months, encountering both boos and autograph seekers. Also, the widow of Custer ("Long Hair") indeed attended multiple performances.

"Coin of the Realm"
>Regarding the head on the so-called Buffalo Nickel, designer James Fraser (1876–1953) said that "my purpose was not to make a portrait but a type," and while he claimed to have used several models, he mentioned by name only Iron Tail (1842–1916), an Oglala Lakota chief, and Two Moon. As for the bison on the back, its model, according to legend, was Black Diamond (1893–1915), who lived his entire life in Central Park Zoo.

HOMELAND SECURITY

"The Mystery of the Barbarity of Charles Graner"
>I used two articles from May 5, 2005: "Abu Ghraib Guard's Ex-Lover Said Told to Humiliate" by Adam Tanner (Reuters) and "Judge Rejects Abuse Plea after Ringleader Testifies" by Ralph Blumenthal (*New York Times*).

Acknowledgments

Many thanks to the editors of the following publications, in which versions of these poems first appeared:

32 Poems: "About Opera," "A Hike in the Headlands"
Able Muse: A Review of Poetry, Prose & Art: "Lauds," "Shades of Tucson"
Cellpoems: "Under the New Regime"
The Cincinnati Review: "Audubon and the Golden Eagle," "Family History," "Keopuolani Eats a Banana," "Wilson and the Ivory Bill"
The Electronic Poetry Review: "The Origin of Chinese Laundry in America," "Overland Wedding"
Encounters: Poems about Race, Ethnicity, and Identity: "Seeing Armstrong"
The Gettysburg Review: "The State of Virginia" (as "The State of Virginia after Southampton")
The Hudson Review: "South of Rome"
Literary Imagination: "Cowboys and Indians," "Mr. Cook's Day"
The New Criterion: "One Morning"
The New Ohio Review: "Dispatches from the Interior"
Poem-A-Day from the Academy of American Poets: "Trip Hop"
Poetry: "Bryant Park at Dusk," "Homeland Security," "The Nights," "Two Moon to a Journalist after Rehearsal"
Poetry International: "Laiku," "Audubon and the Passenger Pigeon: 1831"
Poetry Northwest: "Monroe's Doctrine"
The Rumpus: "King"
Sewanee Review: "James Daniel Brock at Cold Harbor" (as "Cold Harbor")
The Southeast Review: "The Tallahassee of Other Days" (as "Tallahassee These Days")
The Southern Review: "Frank Haskell at Gettysburg" (as "Haskell at Gettysburg")
Subtropics: "Confluence," "Day of Settlement" (as "Flesh of John Brown's Flesh"), "The Mystery of the Barbarity of Charles Graner" (as "Charles Graner Is Not America"), "Wilson & the Carolina Parakeet"
Two Weeks: A Digital Anthology of Contemporary Poetry: "Concordances"

My thanks, too, to David Ward and the National Portrait Gallery, for commissioning the ten-poem sequence "Staring Back at Us," which first appeared in *Lines in Long Array: A Civil War Commemoration*, and to the editors of the following publications, for republishing many of these poems:

Alhambra Poetry Calendar (2008, 2010, 2011, 2013), *American Poets Against the War*; *Best American Poetry 2007*; *The City*; *Creative Writer's Handbook* (5th Edition); *From the Fishhouse: An Anthology of Poems that Sing, Rhyme, Resound, Syncopate, Alliterate, and Just Plain Sound Great*; *From the Fishhouse: An Audio Archive of Emerging Poets*; *The Mind's Eye: A Liberal Arts Journal*; *My Vocabulary* (KSDT radio), *Poem-of-the-Day Podcast* (Poetry Foundation); *Poems from the American South*, *Poetry Daily*, *Poetry International*, *The Rumpus Original Poetry Anthology*, *The Swallow Anthology of New American Poets*.

Over the past decade or so I've received a great deal of support for the writing of this book. I'm grateful to the University of Arkansas for granting me a sabbatical at a crucial stage and to the following organizations for grants and fellowships: The American Antiquarian Society, The Florida Arts Council, The Arizona Commission on the Arts, The National Endowment for the Arts, Stanford University's Wallace Stegner Program, and The Cullman Center for Scholars & Writers at the New York Public Library. I'm also deeply grateful to Heather McHugh for choosing my manuscript for the Anthony Hecht Prize; I was lucky to find her as a reader. Thanks, too, to Philip Hoy and Joseph Harrison of Waywiser Press, whose list I am proud to join. And I owe deep debts to the many wonderful readers, teachers, and friends whose advice and encouragement have helped this book take shape, especially Sidney Wade, Randall Mann, Andrew Shields, Marilyn Nelson, Don Bogen, W.S. Di Piero, Kenneth Fields, Eavan Boland, Camille Dungy, Rosanna Warren, Christian Wiman, Richard Kenney, William Logan, Ilya Kaminsky, Kathleen DuVal, and John DuVal. Finally, my greatest gratitude goes to my family, especially my parents Van Brock and Frances Brock, my in-laws Vis and Bhuvana Viswanathan, and above all Padma Viswanathan, who is my first and last and deepest reader, in art as in life.

A Note About the Author

Geoffrey Brock was born in Atlanta and grew up in Tallahassee, Florida. He received a PhD in comparative literature from the University of Pennsylvania, an MFA in poetry from the University of Florida, and was a Wallace Stegner fellow in poetry at Stanford. His first book, *Weighing Light*, received the New Criterion Poetry Prize and his poems and translations have appeared in journals including *Poetry*, *The New England Review*, *Subtropics*, *Cincinnati Review*, and *Hudson Review*, and in anthologies such as *The Swallow Anthology of New American Poets*, *Best American Poetry 2007*, and *Pushcart Prize XXXIV*. He has received fellowships from the NEA, The Academy of American Poets, The Cullman Center for Scholars & Writers at the New York Public Library, and the Guggenheim Foundation. Brock is also the editor of *The FSG Book of 20th-Century Italian Poetry* and the translator of Cesare Pavese's *Disaffections: Complete Poems 1930-1950*. He teaches at the University of Arkansas in Fayetteville.

A Note About the Author

A Note About the Anthony Hecht Poetry Prize

The Anthony Hecht Poetry Prize was inaugurated in 2005 and is awarded on an annual basis to the best first or second collection of poems submitted. For further information, please visit Waywiser's website at

http://waywiser-press.com/hechtprize.html

FIRST ANNUAL HECHT PRIZE
Judge: J. D. McClatchy
Winner: Morrie Creech, *Field Knowledge*

SECOND ANNUAL HECHT PRIZE
Judge: Mary Jo Salter
Winner: Erica Dawson, *Big-Eyed Afraid*

THIRD ANNUAL HECHT PRIZE
Judge: Richard Wilbur
Winner: Rose Kelleher, *Bundle o' Tinder*

FOURTH ANNUAL HECHT PRIZE
Judge: Alan Shapiro
Winner: Carrie Jerrell, *After the Revival*

FIFTH ANNUAL HECHT PRIZE
Judge: Rosanna Warren
Winner: Matthew Ladd, *The Book of Emblems*

SIXTH ANNUAL HECHT PRIZE
Judge: James Fenton
Winner: Mark Kraushaar, *The Uncertainty Principle*

SEVENTH ANNUAL HECHT PRIZE
Judge: Mark Strand
Winner: Chris Andrews, *Lime Green Chair*

EIGHTH ANNUAL HECHT PRIZE
Judge: Charles Simic
Winner: Shelley Puhak, *Guinevere in Baltimore*

A Note About the Anthony Hecht Poetry Prize

NINTH ANNUAL HECHT PRIZE
Judge: Heather McHugh
Winner: Geoffrey Brock, *Voices Bright Flags*

Other Books from Waywiser

Other Books from Waywiser

Richard Wilbur, *Anterooms*
Richard Wilbur, *Mayflies*
Richard Wilbur, *Collected Poems 1943-2004*
Norman Williams, *One Unblinking Eye*
Greg Williamson, *A Most Marvelous Piece of Luck*

FICTION

Gregory Heath, *The Entire Animal*
Mary Elizabeth Pope, *Divining Venus*
K. M. Ross, *The Blinding Walk*
Gabriel Roth, *The Unknowns**
Matthew Yorke, *Chancing It*

ILLUSTRATED

Nicholas Garland, *I wish ...*
Eric McHenry and Nicholas Garland, *Mommy Daddy Evan Sage*

NON-FICTION

Neil Berry, *Articles of Faith: The Story of British Intellectual Journalism*
Mark Ford, *A Driftwood Altar: Essays and Reviews*
Richard Wollheim, *Germs: A Memoir of Childhood*

* Co-published with Picador